MEMORIES OF MEXICO ALBUM

A COLLECTION OF MEXICO'S MOST POPULAR MELODIES
WITH
ENGLISH AND ORIGINAL SPANISH TEXT

CONTENTS

EDWARD B. MARKS MUSIC COMPANY

EXCLUSIVELY DISTRIBUTED BY
HAL•LEONARD CORPORATION
7777 W. BLUEMOUND RD. P.O. BOX 13819 MILWAUKEE, WI 53213

ALLA EN EL RANCHO GRANDE
My Ranch

English Lyrics by
BARTLEY COSTELLO

Tune Uke
G C E A

Spanish Lyrics & Music by
SILVANO R. RAMOS

I love to roam out yon-der, Oat where the Buf-f'lo
A - llá en el ran-cho gran-de, A - llá don-de vi -

wan - der, _____ Free as the Eag-le fly-ing, I'm
vi - a, _____ Ha - bia u-na ran-che ri - ta Que a -

*) Symbols are for Banjo or Guitar

3rd Verse

Some-times the winter storms tearing,
Set all the cattle a-raring,
But when the winter is over,
We're sure enough in the clover.

Nunca te fíes de promesas
Ni mucho menos de amores
Que si te dan calabzas
Verás lo que son ardores.

4th Verse

Give me the wide open spaces,
That's just where I know my place is,
I love the Ro-de-o dearly,
And the Big Round-Up yearly.

Pon muy atento el oido
Cuando rechine la puerta
Hay muertos que no hacen ruido
Y son muy gordas sus penas.

5th Verse

Tho' we play seven eleven,
My Ranch is next door to Heaven,
We smile when we take a beatin',
But hang a rat when he's cheatin'.

Cuando te pidan cigarro
No des cigarro y cerillo
Porque si das las dos cosas
Te tantearán de zorrillo.

LA CUCARACHA
(The Mexican Cockroach Song)

English Text by
STANLEY ADAMS

Arranged by PAUL HILL

For it looked so ap - pe - tiz - ing, With the bat - ter slow - ly ris - ing,
'Till he saw a sleeve wide o - pen, Snug and warm as he was hop - in',
And he tumb - led nev - er think - ing, In the soup and start - ed sink - ing,
Le pi - di - oa la Vir - gen pu - ra, Di - ne - ro pa - ra gas - tar;

To the edge he start - ed skip - ping, Then he found that he was slip - ping
'Twas the time and place for nap - ping, 'Till some - bod - y start - ed slap - ping,
Oh the cook be - gan to hol - ler, Grabbed the but - ler by the col - lar,
Un pa - na - de - ro - fue - a - mi - sa, No en con - tran - do que - re - zar;

In the pie so hot and blaz - in', Now he's just an - oth - er rais - in. La Cu - ca - rais - in.
Woe be - tide the lit - tle mid - get, He had made the own - er fid - get. La Cu - ca - fid - get.
Out the win - dow went the plat - ter, But our lit - tle friend was fat - ter. La Cu - ca - fat - ter.
Le pi - di - oa la Vir - gen pu - ra, Di - ne - ro pa - ra gas - tar.— La Cu - ca - tar.—

D.S. al Fine %   Fine

CODA

La Cu - ca - ra - cha, La Cu - ca - ra - cha, Just the same as you and
La Cu - ca - ra - cha, La Cu - ca - ra - cha, Ya no pue - de ca - mi -

I, He got the jit - ters, the sweets and bit - ters, Lived and loved and said "good - bye."
nar, Por - que no tie - ne, por - que le fal - ta, Ma - ri - hua - na que fu - mar.

4.

La Cucaracha, La Cucaracha,
Woke up on election day,
La Cucaracha, La Cucaracha,
Heard the things they had to say,
A lot of lying and alibing,
Empty heads without a plan,
La Cucaracha, La Cucaracha,
Said, "I'm glad I'm not a man?"

REFRAIN

Then one day he saw an army,
Said,"The drums and bugle charm me,
Still if all the world are brothers,
Why should these men fight the others?
Guess it's just for love and glory,
Who'd believe another story?
These are men so brave and plucky,
Look at me, boy am I lucky!"

5.

La Cucaracha, La Cucaracha,
Wondered where his love could be,
La Cucaracha, La Cucaracha,
Wandered on so mis'rably.
The bees and beetles and old boll weevils,
Chased him off with many "Scats",
First they would scold him and then they told him,
They were bug aristocrats.

REFRAIN

Then one day while in the garden,
He just said, "I beg your pardon",
To a lady Cucaracha,
And he added, "Now I've gótcha".
She was coy but she was willing,
And for years their love was thrilling,
They still meet at half past seven,
Up in Cucaracha heaven.

La Cucaracha, La Cucaracha,
Just the same as you and I,
He got the jitters, the sweets and bitters,
Lived and loved and said "Goodbye."

LA BORRACHITA
(There Is No One Like You)

English Lyric by
CAROL RAVEN

Spanish Lyric by
IGNACIO FERNANDEZ ESPERON

Tune Ukulele
G C E A

Music by
IGNACIO FERNANDEZ ESPERON

*) Symbols are for Banjo or Guitar

you,_____ When stars are burn - - ing, Love comes to hu - man hearts,_____
*er,*_____ *Di - jo que no,*_____ *Que si ha-bia de llo - rar,*_____

____And leaves them yearn - ing, There is no one like you,_____ I long for your ca-
Pa - que vol - ver. *Bo - rra-chi-ta me voy,*_____ *Has-ta la - ca-pi-*

ress - es,_____When I wan-der with you, In the won-der-ful hush of the dew.
*tal,*_____ *Pa ser-vir-al pa-trón,* *Que me man-dó lla-mar an-tea-yer.*

dew._____
*yer.*_____

DONDE ESTAS CORAZON
Where Are You, My Heart

English Version by
MARJORIE HARPER

Spanish Lyrics and Music
By L. MARTINEZ SERRANO
Arranged by J. Rosamond Johnson

CHORUS

Oh! where are you, my heart?_____ For your throb-bing is still!_____
*Don de es-tás co-ra-zón,*_____ *No oi-go tu pal-pi-tar,*_____

Since our Fate bade us part,_____ Life is emp-ty and chill._____ I am long-ing to
*Es tan gran-de el do-lor,*_____ *Que no pue-de llo-rar.*_____ *Yo qui-sie-ra llo-*

cry,_____ But the tears will not start._____ Our deep love on-ly
*rar,*_____ *Y no ten-go más llan-to.*_____ *La que-ri-a yo*

Death could de-ny! Oh, where are you my heart?_____ heart?_____
tan-to y se fué, *Pa-ra nun-ca tor-nar.*_____ *-nar.*_____

POPULAR JARABE TAPATIO

F. A. PARTICHELA
Arranged by J. Rosamond Johnson

LAS GAVIOTAS
SEAGULLS

English Lyric by
CAROL RAVEN

Arranged by
PAUL HILL

Allegro moderato

VOICE

Di - me ne - gra, por
It was sum - mer, the
And though nev - er a

Al Coda

que no me a - mas, Tu e - res mi vi - da, mi bien - es - tar,____
day was dy - ing, The sea - gulls fly - ing a - cross the sea;____
girl was sweet - er, Than my A - ni - ta, I left her free;____

Ab   dim   Bb7

*) Symbols and Diagrams are for Guitar

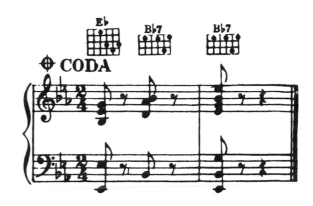

ne la mar._____
*said "no, no."*_____
*way from love.*_____

Ya las gaviotas tienden su vuelo,
Abren sus alas para volar,
Andan buscando nidos de amores,
Nidos de amores encontrarán.

Es muy bonito tener amore
En otras tierras que Dios formó,
Dame un abrazo, dame un besito,
Para vivir más contento yo.

Bellas gaviotas que andan volando,
Que andan volando sobre del mar,
Buscan gozozas nuevos amores,
Nuevos amores que han de encontrar.

Eres hermosa, cual una rosa,
Como las flores que hay en mi hogar,
Jardín de flores de mil colores,
Que ni las conchas que hay en la mar.

Joven hermosa, si tu quisieras,
En fragil lancha irte a pasear,
Para contarte mis sufrimientos,
Los que he pasado allá en altamar.

No cabe duda que eres ingrata,
No cabe duda que eres infiel,
Amas el oro, amas la plata,
Eres amiga del interés.

Mira negra, vente conmigo,
En mi barquilla y lo verás,
Dame un besito, dame un abrazo,
Mientras yo duerma tú remarás.

Mira nena, vente conmigo,
En mi barquilla te llevaré,
Y cuando estemos en la otra orilla,
Nuevas canciones te cantaré.

Ya me despido, querida joven,
Ya me despido sin dilación,
Pues te lo juro que aunque esté lejos,
Nunca te cambio por otro amor.

Todos los astros que hay en el cielo,
Si por la noche los ves brillar,
Muestran las conchas flotando en la agua,
En lo profundo del ancho mar.

Joven hermosa si tú me amaras,
Y me quisieras como yo a ti.
Yo te daría mi alma y mi vida,
Y adoraríate con frenesí.

Desde el momento en que yo te vi,
Loco he quedado de puro amor,
Y desde entonces, hermosa joven,
Por ti suspira mi corazón.

NEGRA CONSENTIDA
MY PET BRUNETTE

English Version by
MARJORIE HARPER
Arranged by J. Rosamond Johnson

Spanish Version and Music by
JOAQUIN PARDAVÉ

A. Wagner & Levien

LA CHAPARRITA

(Adios Beloved)

English Lyrics by
FRANCIA LUBAN

Tune Ukulele:
G C E A

Music by
IGNATIO FERNANDEZ ESPERON
Arr. by Rosamond Johnson

*)Symbols are for Banjo or Guitar

NOCHE AZUL
(BLUE NIGHT)

English Lyrics by
MARJORIE HARPER
Spanish Lyrics by
J. S. ESPINOSA de los MONTEROS

Music by
CARLOS ESPINOSA de los MONTEROS
Arranged by J. Rosamond Johnson

Sweet im-age, I long for you,
Be - lla i-ma-gen que so-ñé,

Love - ly as the night of blue._____ Can't
En mis no-ches de do-lor,_____ Men

A. Wagner & Levien   *) Symbols and Diagrams are for Guitar

THE SWALLOW
(La Golondrina)

English Lyrics by
MARJORIE HARPER

Arranged by
J. ROSAMOND JOHNSON

VERSE

Beloved bird, my fellow pilgrim winging,
  I hear thee singing, as I sang of old!
If it should be,
That thou should come with me,
I shall make for thee,
  A haven from the cold!

CHORUS

Small swallow flying,
The storms of the winter defying,
Where art thou plying?
  Tell me, where dost thou go?
Where'er thou art,
Now I pledge thee my heart,
As this day I part,
  With ev'ry joy I know!

Adonde irá veloz y fatigada
La golondrina que de aqui se vá.
O si en el viento se hallará extraviada
Buscando abrigo y no lo encontrará.
Junto a mi lecho le pondré su nido
En donde pueda la estación pasar;
Tambien yo estoy en la región perdido
Oh cielo santo! y sin poder volar.

Dejé también mi patria idolatrada,
Esa mansion que me miró nacer,
Mi vida es hoy errante y angustiada
I ya no puedo á mi mansión volver.
Ave querida, amada peregrina,
Mi corazón al tuyo estrecharé,
Oiré tu canto, tierna golondrina,
Recordaré mi patria y lloraré.

CANCION MIXTECA
(Wondering)

English Lyrics by
BARTLEY COSTELLO
Arr. by PAUL HILL

Spanish Words and
Music by
JOSÉ LÓPEZ ALAVÉZ

LAS MAÑANITAS
(Good Morning)

English Lyrics by
CAROL RAVEN

TUNE UKE
A D F♯ B

Arranged by
PAUL HILL

Darl-ing wake! The shad-ows fly, The sleep-y moon has said good-
Es - tas son las ma - ña - ni tas que can - ta - ba el Rey Da-

bye, Come and greet the rose of dawn-ing, And say good morn-ing to
vid, Pe - ro no e - ran tan bo - ni - tas, Co-mo las can - tan a -

me. On the streets the lights are out, Lamp-light-er knows what he's a-
qui. Si el se - re - no de la es-qui - na me qui - sie - ra ha-cer fa-

THE DOVE
LA PALOMA

English Lyrics by
MARJORIE HARPER

Music by
S. de YRADIER
Arr. by
J. Rosamond Johnson

2.

I'll give you my hand, with all of the love I own;

I'll live all my life for you and you alone;

We'll go to church for blessings that wait in store,

And so - there'll be one where two had been before.

3.

The day we are married, we'll tell the world "Goodbye,"

Away we will go together, you and I.

But when time has passed us by with each coming year,

'Tis then, many little Gauchos will appear.

2.

El dia que nos casemos
Valgame Dios!
En la semana que hay ir
Me hace reir
Desde la Yglesia juntitos
Que si senor
Nos hiremos a dormir
Alla voy yó
Si a tu ventana llega etc.

3.

Cuando el curita nos seche
La bendicion
En la Yglesia Catrédal
Alla voy yó
Yo te duré la manita
Con mucho amor
Y el cura dos hisopazos
Que si senor
Si a tu ventana llega etc.

HASTIO
Love Shy
(Canción)

Lyric by
AL SILVERMAN

Music by
MARÍA TERESA de LARA
Arranged by AGUSTÍN LARA

HIMNO NACIONAL MEXICANO
(Mexican National Hymn)

Arranged
by
PAUL HILL

Music
by
JAIME NUNO

48